KU-719-737

How Is Art Made?

Elizabeth Newbery

Belitha Press

First published in Great Britain in 2001 by

Ⓒ Belitha Press
  A member of Chrysalis Books Plc.
64 Brewery Road, London N7 9NT

Copyright © Belitha Press 2001
Concept and text copyright © Elizabeth Newbery 2001

Editors: Claire Edwards, Kate Phelps
Designer: Jane Horne
Picture researcher: Diana Morris
Consultant: Anthea Peppin
Education consultant: Sue Lacey

ISBN 1 84138 198 5

British Library Cataloguing-in-Publication Data for
this book is available from the British Library.

Printed in Hong Kong

Picture acknowledgements

Cover:
Galleria dell'Accademia, Venice/Bridgeman Art Library: front cover cr.
Private Collection/Christies/Bridgeman Art Library: front cover cl. Private
Collection/Werner Forman Archive: front cover bl. Keren Su/Stone: front
cover br. Victoria &Albert Museum, London/Bridgeman Art Library: front
cover c.
Scottish National Gallery of Modern Art/Bridgeman Art Library: back cover
© Lichtenstein Estate/DACS London 2001.
Inside:
Arts Council Collection of Great Britain/Bridgeman Art Library: 26-7 © the
artist. Ashmolean Museum, Oxford/Bridgeman Art Library: 27tr. Morton
Beebe/Corbis: 23b © the artist. Chris Beetles Gallery, London/Bridgeman
Art Library: 15tl © the artist.British Museum/Bridgeman Art Library: 4b.
Christies, London/Bridgeman Art Library: 20-21 © DACS London 2001.
Andy Cox/Stone: 20bl. Gary Fabriano/Sipa/Rex Features: 5tr © the artist.
The Flemming-Wyfold Art Foundation/Bridgeman Art Library: 11b © the
artist. Fogg Art Museum/Harvard Art Gallery/Bridgeman Art Library: 11t ©
the artist. Galleria dell'Accademia, Venice/Bridgeman Art Library: 15c. Leslie
Garland:19tl © the artist. Grotte de Peche Merle/Index/Bridgeman Art
Library: 1b, 10c, 29b. Hermitage, St Petersburg/Bridgeman Art Library: 19tr.
John Lawrence/Powerstock/Zefa: 7bl. Wally McNamee/Corbis: 27br.
Metropolitan Museum, New York/Bridgeman Art Library: 8cr, 28t. Gift of

the City of Montreux, Switzerland, Detroit Renaissance, and the artist/Detroit
Institute of Arts: 21br © DACS London 2001. National Galleries of
Scotland/Bridgeman Art Library: 7cr © Lichtenstein Estate/DACS London
2001. National Gallery, London/Bridgeman Art Library: 7tl. National Gallery
of Art, Washington DC: 3t & 17t © Les Hériteurs Matisse/DACS London
2001. Philadelphia Museum of Art/Corbis: 13b © the artist. Private
Collection/Bonhams, London/Bridgeman Art Library: 12b, 23c © the artist.
Private Collection/Bridgeman Art Library: 6br, 13tl ©   the artist, 17b © the
artist, 23t © the artist,   25t © the artist, 25b © DACS London 2001. Private
Collection/Christies/Bridgeman Art Library: 18r. Private Collection/Werner
Forman Archive: 4-5c. G Ryan & S Beyer/Stone: 5br. San Francesco,
Arrezzo/Bridgeman Art Library: 9b. Paul Seheult/Eye Ubiquitous: 22b.
Sheffield Galleries & Museums Trust, UK/Bridgeman Art Library: 9t © the
artist. Stockmarket/Corbis: 15b. Keren Su/Stone: 14b. Tretyakov Gallery,
Moscow/Bridgeman Art Library: 16b. Victoria &Albert Museum,
London/Bridgeman Art Library: 24t. Peter Willi/Louvre/Bridgeman Art
Library: 2br, 19br.

Every attempt has been made to clear copyrights but should there be
inadvertent omissions please apply to the publisher for rectification.

**Some of the more unfamiliar words used
in this book are explained in the glossary
on pages 30 and 31.**

Contents

What do you like using to make a picture?
Colourful felt-tips? Messy paint? Or something else?
Once, artists chose materials that lasted a long time.
Today, they can choose anything they like!

What a

People used to think that works of art had to be made of expensive materials by the best artists and craftworkers. In Ancient Egypt craftsmen made masks of solid gold inlaid with blue glass and precious jewels for pharaohs' mummies. In India, rare jade was carved into bowls and ornaments for rulers. At the beginning of the twentieth century, many new materials allowed artists and craftspeople more choice. Today, artists can choose to work with anything they like – from stone to space-age materials.

◄ *Vandal on horseback, mosaic from Carthage made about AD 500*
This mosaic was made in Roman times. Mosaics are pictures made by fixing small pieces of marble, pottery or glass (called tesserae) into cement-like material.

Bird from Peru, made between 200 BC and AD 650
A goldsmith made this bird in Peru, South America, about 2,000 years ago. It is made of beaten gold and has eyes and feathers decorated with a semi-precious stone called turquoise.

Puppy by Jeff Koons, 1992 ▲
Jeff Koons makes sculptures of ready-made items. But he makes them giant-sized and in unusual materials such as stainless steel. This dog, modelled on a cuddly toy, is made of flowers.

choice!

Ice carving, about 1990 ▶
This glass-like sculpture was carved out of blocks of ice for the Winter Festival at St Paul, Minnesota, USA. How long do you think it lasted?

Paint is colour (called pigment) mixed with liquid (called binder). It has been used for painting pictures since the earliest times when it was made of coloured earths. Modern paints still have natural materials in them, but chemicals are added to make them tougher.

What is paint?

Prehistoric people mixed coloured earth and burnt materials together with blood, animal fat or beeswax to make paint. The Romans imported purple made from crushed shells and made red from a mineral called cinnabar. In the Middle Ages monks used tempera, paint made from earth and minerals mixed with egg or glue. Later in the Middle Ages, artists used oil paints mixed with oil from seeds and nuts. Today, artists also use acrylic paint made from chemicals.

▶ *The Invention of Oil Paint, engraving from about 1600*
Artists once mixed paint by hand. These two assistants are grinding pigment and mixing it with oil on a stone slab.

◀ *The Arnolfini Portrait*
by Jan van Eyck, 1434
Jan van Eyck was one of the first artists to make good use of oil paint. The oils can be used thick or thin. Van Eyck liked to build up thin, transparent layers that made the colours glow and shine.

In the Car ▶
by Roy Lichtenstein, 1963
Modern artists can use any type of paint they like. In this painting Roy Lichtenstein used magna, which is an industrial paint normally used for cars. Do you think it would be as effective if he had painted it in oil paints?

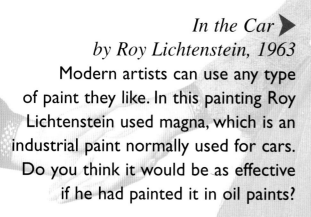

◀ *Making paint*
Today, paint is made in a factory. Modern paints are tested to make sure they are safe to use and hard-wearing. Here paint is being put in a machine to see what will happen to colours in strong sunlight.

Artists can use anything they like to paint with – fine brushes, giant decorators' brushes, knives, fingers and even feet. They can paint on any surface as long as the paint sticks to it.

Tools of the

Artists pick the tools they use and the surfaces they paint on very carefully. Painters who choose watercolours use thick, absorbent paper to soak up the water and good-quality brushes made of animal hair. Artists who paint with oil paint sometimes squeeze it straight out of the tube or spread it on with knives. Oil paints can be applied to canvas, wood or board but the surface has to be primed. This means it has to be treated with a thin coat of size (glue) and then with white paint to help the paint stick to the surface.

Mummy Portrait of a Boy with an Injured Eye, ▲
from Fayum, Egypt, about AD 138–161
This portrait was painted nearly 2,000 years ago by a method that has kept the colours looking very fresh. Pigment was mixed with hot, melted wax and painted on to wood. When the picture was complete it was gently heated so that the paint and the wood bonded together.

Looking towards Mornington Crescent Station, Night by Frank Auerbach, 1973
Frank Auerbach uses thick brushes, palette knives and even his fingers to build up layers of thick, gooey oil paint called impasto. He paints over his pictures many times.

▼ *The Queen of Sheba, a fresco by Piero della Francesca, about 1452–1457*
A fresco is a type of wall painting that is painted straight on to fresh, damp plaster. The word 'fresco' is the Italian word for fresh. Artists needed great skill to paint frescos. They could only paint on the plaster when it was damp, so could only do a bit at a time. If they made a mistake, they had to remove the plaster and start again.

trade

Paint can be splashed, sploshed, splattered, sponged or stencilled! The way an artist paints depends on the effect he or she wants to achieve.

The famous American artist, Jackson Pollock, liked to use cheap household paint. He dribbled, flicked and splattered it straight out of the can on to a giant canvas laid on the floor. Today, many artists like to experiment with different ways of putting on paint such as spraying, stencilling, sponging, rolling, dripping and even throwing it on. They can also paint on different surfaces, such as paper, board, wood, canvas and sheets of metal, to make the paint react in different ways. But these ideas are not new – in prehistoric times people sprayed paint on to rock.

Good

▲ *Hand stencil from Grotte de Pech Merle, France, made about 24,000–20,000 BC*
This stencil of a hand was made about 25,000 years ago by someone who sprayed paint over their hand laid on a rock. They may have put the paint in their mouth and blown it out in a fine spray or blown it through a small hollow bone.

Blue Veil
by Morris Louis, 1958–1959
Morris Louis was interested
in what paint could do rather
than what he could paint with
it. He mixed water with acrylic
paints to make it very thin.
Then he poured it on to
untreated canvas. The paint
spread out and stained the
canvas in unexpected ways.

effects

◀ *Cat and Flowers*
by Elizabeth
Blackadder, 1981
This artist adds lots
of water to make
the watercolour paint
thinner so that
she can get very
delicate effects.

Do you have to use paint to paint a picture? Some artists don't think so. They think other materials allow them greater freedom to paint what they want and how they want. Some use paint but add other materials too to create a particular effect.

Adding

Adding other materials to paint is not a new idea. In Europe in the Middle Ages, monks copied out the pages of the Bible by hand and decorated them with gold beaten paper-thin. Using precious materials was a way of honouring God. In India, the royal court painters added gold to small paintings (called miniatures) commissioned by princes and other rulers. Today, artists often add other materials to give different textures. The American artist Jackson Pollock sometimes added broken glass or sand to give the paint a rough feel.

▲ *Illuminated manuscript from Mogul India, about 1600*
This delicate pattern is decorated with gold, ink and paint. It comes from a page of a book called *The Garden of Truth* by Hakim Sana'i.

◀ Cracked Mud Study with Bird, Dog and Tyre Tracks. From Lorry Park Series by Mark Boyle, 1979

Mark Boyle chooses what he paints and the materials he uses in an unusual way. He sticks a pin in a map and goes to that place. Then he throws a right-angle tool over his shoulder. Wherever it lands he makes an exact copy of that spot with the materials he finds there. In this picture, the place was a muddy lorry park and the exact spot included marks made by tyres, birds and dogs. He has recreated the spot using mud, grit, rubbish and fibreglass.

to paint

▶ Gingko by Sigmar Polke, twentieth century

Sigmar Polke uses dangerous materials such as chemicals, varnishes, poisonous materials and solvents in his paintings! The materials react with one another and alter the surface. Sometimes changes even cause the painting to fall apart. Polke thinks that watching changes taking place is an important part of making his works of art.

All sorts of people draw. Architects draw plans for buildings. Teachers draw diagrams to explain how things work. Archaeologists record objects they dig up by drawing them. And people give directions to others by drawing maps.

Drawing

Drawing is best described as making marks or lines, usually on paper. Drawing lines can be made with anything that makes a mark – felt-tips, crayons, hard pencils, ink, chalks, sticks of charcoal, soft powdery pastels, a stick in sand or a feather dipped in paint. Many artists use drawing as a way of learning more about a place, an animal or a person. Others try out new ideas by making quick sketches in a sketchbook. Later, they may use them in another work of art. Sometimes artists make trial drawings, called cartoons, before starting a large painting.

▶ *Chinese calligrapher*
This Chinese man has been specially trained to make beautiful letters, called calligraphy. He chooses a fine bamboo brush and ink to draw with.

◀ Dick Whittington and his cat by Quentin Blake, 1989
Quentin Blake illustrates children's books with drawings. He likes to draw very quickly and often chooses pen and ink. Here he has added grey watercolour paint.

it out

▶ Detail of Seven Studies of Grotesque Faces by Leonardo da Vinci, fifteenth century
Leonardo da Vinci liked to draw with pen and ink. This drawing of a face was done in pen and ink, shaded with chalk. He made drawings throughout his life of everything from studies of plants, animals and the human body to ideas for weapons, buildings and flying machines.

◀ Pavement artist, Bristol, England
You have probably seen pavement artists at work in big cities. They usually make copies of well-known paintings in coloured chalks that are cleaned off each day. This artist is making a copy of *Mona Lisa* by Leonardo da Vinci, one of the most famous paintings in the world.

Some pictures are made by sticking down materials to make an image. Artists have used all sorts of things from old bus tickets, corks, feathers and fabric to large bits of metal and old car parts.

Stick 'em up!

A rtists made the first collages in France in the early twentieth century. They named this form of art 'collage' from the French word *coller*, meaning to stick or glue. Different papers, tickets, photographs and other everyday objects were stuck to paintings. In the 1960s, American artists began to use much larger materials, such as sheets of metal, which were welded, nailed or screwed on.

▲ *Italian Still Life by Lyubov Popova, 1914*
Lyubov Popova was one of the first artists to experiment with collage. For example, she often glued pieces of cardboard to the canvas so that shapes projected outwards. In this picture she used oil paint, paper and gypsum (a chalky mineral).

▲ *Large composition with masks
by Henri Matisse, 1953*
When Henri Matisse was 70,
he became very ill and could no
longer paint with a brush. But that
didn't stop him making pictures.
Instead of painting, he cut shapes out
of coloured paper and moved them
about on huge canvases with a stick
before gluing them down. This was
one of the last pictures Matisse
made before he died.

◄ *Tadpole
by Robert Rauschenberg, 1963*
Robert Rauschenberg, an American
artist, was one of the first artists to
make works of art in more unusual
materials. Here he has used paint, part
of a car tyre and a strip of metal nailed
on to a picture of an American city.
Would you describe it as a painting,
a collage or a relief (see page 19)?

Sculptures are three-dimensional works of art. All kinds of materials from hard stone to soft clay are cut, formed and moulded to make shapes. You can walk round sculptures, touch them and even walk through some of them.

What a

Until the twentieth century, sculpture was usually made in one of two ways. Hard material such as stone or wood was cut away or carved. Soft material such as clay was built up round a frame, called an armature. Then it was cast to make it longer lasting. To cast a sculpture, the sculptor first made a mould from the model. Material such as melted bronze or wet plaster was poured into the mould. When it had set, the mould was broken away. Many sculptors still make sculpture in this way. Today, artists also use all kinds of materials and methods to make sculpture.

▶ *Little Dancer, aged 14*
by Edgar Degas, 1881
Edgar Degas made sculptures to try out ideas. He didn't intend them to last a long time so he carved many of them out of soft wax supported on armatures made of cork. Many of the sculptures were cast in bronze after Degas died.

*The Angel of the North
by Anthony Gormley, 1998*
Sculptors think carefully about where sculpture
will be placed and from what angle people will
see it. This huge sculpture was specially
designed to be seen from a long
way away. The people in this
photograph give you some
idea how big the
sculpture really is.

A fly eating a pear,
Japanese netsuke, nineteenth century
This tiny sculpture, made over a hundred
years ago, is about as big as a conker.
It is a netsuke (say net sooki), a toggle carved
from wood. Rich Japanese men used netsuke to
decorate the ends of the cords that held
pouches to the sashes of kimonos.

carve
up!

*The Stele of Pharsalos, made in
Ancient Greece, about 450 BC*
When is a sculpture not a sculpture? When
it's a relief! You can't walk round a relief,
but it is not completely flat like a painting.
This relief was once part of a building. It was
carved out of marble about 2,500 years ago.

Many sculptors like to make sculpture that moves. Some is designed to hang from ceilings, some to stand on floors. Moving sculpture is set in motion by wind, motor or touch. It's art plus science and technology!

Moving

Sculpture that moves is called kinetic art (from the Greek word *kinetikos* meaning to move). Some artists are interested in energy and the way sculpture can be made to change shape if it moves, for example, by floating in liquid. Many modern artists use projectors and sound recordings so that kinetic art becomes a mixture of light, sound and movement.

◀ *Baby playing with a mobile*
A mobile is one kind of moving sculpture, or kinetic art. Shapes appear to change and shadows and patterns of light are thrown on to floors, ceilings and walls. This is why babies find mobiles hanging over their cots so fascinating. Do you think this baby's mobile is a kinetic sculpture?

◀ *Untitled by Alexander Calder, twentieth century*
Alexander Calder was an engineer before he became an artist. He made simple, beautifully balanced, often giant-sized mobiles. They use only currents of air to make them move gently round. The simple shapes, cut out of red, yellow or blue metal, cast wonderful patterns of coloured light on the floor, ceiling and walls.

around

O Sole Mio by Jean Tinguely, 1982 ▶
Jean Tinguely was interested in the idea that movement can be harmful as well as good. For instance, he made mobiles that gradually destroy themselves as they move. He used junk, metal and wire to make mobiles that are operated by motors. Sometimes he included sound by making one part strike another.

Land art is working with natural materials and landscapes to make sculptures. Some artists want to make their mark on the land, others want their art to become part of the land.

Land art

Many artists like the idea that their work will last a long time. But land artists are often interested in exploring the way nature will take over, change or wear away works of art if left outside. Some, such as Richard Long, take their ideas from wild, lonely and unspoilt places. He goes for long walks, sometimes making land art. At other times, he collects materials on the journey and builds a sculpture or makes a picture in the gallery later. Because land art doesn't last long and is often built in out-of-the-way places, land artists record it with words, maps, photography or film. They often sell the photographs instead of the land art.

▲ *Sand sculpture*
This little boy is making a face in the sand. He uses seaweed for hair and pebbles for eyes. The tide will come in soon and wash it away. Is the boy a land artist?

*Geneva Circle Two
by Richard Long, 1987*
Richard Long collected
these pieces of stone
while walking in Italy.
Later he made this
circle in a gallery.

*Sycamore leaves stitched together
with stalks hung from a still green oak
by Andy Goldsworthy, 1987*
Andy Goldsworthy likes to use materials
he finds on the land such as stones,
sticks, leaves and even ice. He made this
sculpture from leaves stitched together
with stalks, hung it from an oak tree
and then took this photograph of it.
What do you think he is trying
to say about nature?

*Running Fence
by Christo, 1976*
Christo makes huge,
outsized land art.
This fence snakes its way
for a great distance over
the Californian landscape.
Do you think it helps to
show up the soft colours
and gentle hills which you
might not otherwise see?

When printing was reinvented in Europe 500 years ago, artists realized that they could make many copies of one picture. This meant that many more people could afford to buy art.

Print it off

There are many ways in which to print pictures. Linocuts, woodcuts, potato prints, etchings and engravings are all made by cutting into hard material to leave raised areas. The surface is coated with ink and pressed on to paper to make a print. Lithographs are made by drawing on a stone block with a greasy crayon. The stone is wetted and inked but the ink sticks only to the crayon. Then the block is put on to a machine with a roller that transfers the ink off the stone and on to the paper. Today, many print-makers combine traditional printing methods such as lithography with modern photographic processes.

▲ *Aristide Bruant at Les Ambassadeurs by Henri Toulouse-Lautrec, 1892* In the 1800s, posters were usually lithographs. Henri Toulouse-Lautrec was a painter who also designed posters. He used lithography to make simple but bold designs. They are still some of the best posters ever made.

Buffalo Waking – Lake Kariba by Angela Newberry, twentieth century

Silkscreen printing is made by stretching finely woven fabric over a frame. Shapes are painted on the fabric with waterproof varnish. When ink is pushed through the screen with a rubber blade it can't pass through the varnish, so patterns are left on the cloth beneath. This image has been created in the same way using photographic technology.

Young Girls on a Bridge by Edvard Munch, about 1901

Munch made this woodcut by cutting into a hard block of wood with a sharp steel gouge. Then he covered the wood with ink and pressed it on to paper in a printing press. Notice how he used the lines made by the gouge to make a strong design.

Have you ever visited an art gallery or museum and wondered why the light was so low? Or why there are sometimes 'don't touch' notices near sculptures?

Looking after

Works of art need to be looked after if they are to last a long time. Low lighting helps to protect fragile paintings, drawings and manuscripts from fading or discolouring. 'Don't touch' notices are there to protect sculpture from the natural salts in your hands that cause damage even to tough materials like metal. Works of art sometimes have to be cleaned and repaired by experts, called conservators, who work in studios. Some modern works of art may be difficult to care for because they are made of materials not usually used for works of art – such as chocolate. Others may be made of poor quality materials, such as the sketches made on toilet paper by Stanley Spencer.

▲ *George and the Dragon by Tony Cragg, 1984*
This sculpture is made of plastic, wood, aluminium and wickerwork. It's quite a problem for conservators because each material has to be cleaned, mended and looked after in a different way.

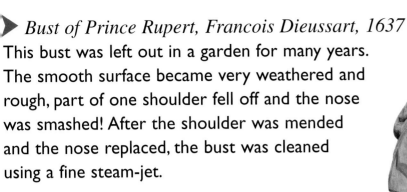

Bust of Prince Rupert, Francois Dieussart, 1637
This bust was left out in a garden for many years.
The smooth surface became very weathered and
rough, part of one shoulder fell off and the nose
was smashed! After the shoulder was mended
and the nose replaced, the bust was cleaned
using a fine steam-jet.

art

Restoring paintings in a studio ▶
When old paintings are cleaned or repaired they
sometimes reveal hidden surprises. When this picture
was x-rayed for damage, another picture was
discovered underneath.

About the artists

▶ *Frank Auerbach* was born in Berlin, Germany, in 1931. He likes to paint the buildings and people around his studio in London.

▶ *Elizabeth Blackadder* was born in Falkirk, Scotland, in 1931. She is best known for delicate watercolours of still-life subjects.

▶ *Quentin Blake* was born in England in 1932. He has illustrated many children's books.

▶ *Mark Boyle* was born in Glasgow, Scotland, in 1934. He is a sculptor as well as a painter and has even made light shows for rock concerts.

▶ *Alexander Calder* was born in Philadelphia, USA, in 1898 and died in 1976. Calder used his knowledge as an engineer to make sculptures.

▶ *Tony Cragg* is a sculptor who was born in Liverpool, England, in 1949. He is interested in industrial products, such as plastic, and the effect they have on our lives.

▶ *Christo* was born in Gabrovo, Bulgaria, in 1935. He is especially well known for huge projects such as wrapping up public buildings in cloth.

▶ *Edgar Degas* was born in Paris, France, in 1834 and died in 1917. Degas studied law before deciding to become a painter. He was very interested in photography and liked to paint 'snapshots' of people taking part in everyday activities.

▶ *Jan van Eyck* was born in the Netherlands but we don't know the exact date. He died in 1441. He was a court painter and a diplomat in Bruges (now in Belgium).

▶ *Andy Goldsworthy* was born in Cheshire, England, in 1956. His land art, *Sycamore leaves*, was made in the Yorkshire Sculpture Park.

▶ *Anthony Gormley* was born in London, England, in 1950. Gormley often uses his own body as a model. *The Angel of the North* can be seen on the hills outside Gateshead, in the north of England.

▶ *Jeff Koons* was born in York, USA, in 1955. He is famous for his outsized sculptures of ready-made items such as toys and ornaments re-made in unexpected materials.

▶ *Leonardo da Vinci* was born Vinci, Italy, in 1452 and died in 1519. He was a sculptor, writer, architect, inventor, scientist and musician as well as a painter.

▶ *Roy Lichtenstein* was born in New York, USA, in 1923 and died in 1997. He is one of the best-known Pop artists, who took their ideas from advertising, comic strips and popular entertainment.

▶ *Richard Long* was born in Bristol, England, in 1945. Nearly all his sculptures are about the long walks he does all over the world.

▶ *Morris Louis* was born in Baltimore, USA, in 1912 and died in 1962. Many of his paintings are experiments with thin layers of paint in which one colour fades into the next.

▶ *Henri Matisse* was born in France in 1869 and died in 1954. He was a painter, sculptor, designer of stage sets and costumes, and he also illustrated books.

▶ *Edvard Munch* was born in Lote, Norway, in 1863 and died in 1944. He suffered from mental illness. His unhappy friendships with women inspired many of his paintings.

▶ *Angela Newberry* was born in England and is a print maker who makes linocuts and screen prints. She is especially interested in subjects about the environment.

▶ *Piero della Francesco* was born in Sansepolcro, Italy, sometime between 1415 and 1420 and died in 1492. He painted frescos and wrote about perspective and geometry.

▶ *Jackson Pollock* was born in Cody, USA, in 1912 and died in 1956. He was famous for his paintings made by pouring paint onto a giant canvas.

▶ *Sigmar Polke* was born in Oels, Germany, in 1941. Many people think he is one of the most original of modern artists.

▶ *Lyubov Popova* was born near Moscow, Russia, in 1889 and died in 1924. She travelled a great deal, but loved traditional Russian architecture and art.

▶ *Robert Rauschenberg* was born in Port Arthur, USA, in 1925. He is one of the most important American artists of the twentieth century and one of the first Pop artists.

▶ *Stanley Spencer* was born in Cookham, England, in 1891 and died in 1959. He took much of his inspiration from the small village where he was born, Cookham in Berkshire.

▶ *Jean Tinguely* was born in Fribourg, Switzerland, in 1925 and died in 1991. Throughout his life he experimented with mechanical sculptures, using motors to make them move. The movements often went wrong with very unpredictable results!

▶ *Henri Toulouse-Lautrec* was born in Albi, France, in 1864 and died in 1901. He liked to paint scenes from music and dance halls, circuses and cafes, and designed some of the best posters that have ever been made.

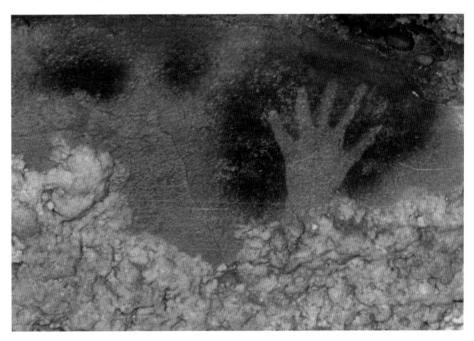

Things to do

Some of these experiments are messy so ask an adult to help you.

Mixing paint *pages 6–7*
Experiment with mixing your own paints. Try grinding charcoal and dry clay with the back of a spoon and mixing with water. Or why not try mixing them with different binders such as wallpaper paste, melted wax or cooking oil?

Different tools *pages 8–9*
Make your own tools to draw and paint with. Try sharpening a twig or hammering the end of it and dipping it in ink. Or you could try dragging a piece of sponge through paint and on to paper.

Paint like Morris Louis *pages 10–11*
You will need runny paint in two or more colours, sheets of watercolour paper (from art shops), a jug and a large container (a roasting tin is good). Pour one colour of paint into a jug. Hold the paper at an angle with one edge in the tray. Pour the paint in a trickle slowly over the paper. Tilt the paper in different directions. Now add a second colour.

Become a land artist *pages 22–23*
Collect twelve pebbles of a similar shape, size or colour and arrange them in a circle. Or collect twelve pebbles ranging from small to large, or from dark-grey to light-grey, and arrange them in order in a line.

Glossary

acrylic paints Paints made of chemicals.

aluminium A silvery-white metal.

archaeologist Someone who studies the past by looking at old objects and ruins.

architect Someone who designs buildings.

armature A framework used to support a sculpture.

bronze A golden-brown metal mainly made from copper and tin. It is used to cast sculpture.

bust A sculpture of the head and shoulders.

calligraphy The art of beautiful writing.

canvas A coarse cloth which artists use to paint on.

cartoon A trial drawing for a larger work of art.

cast A shape made by pouring liquid metal or plaster into a hollow mould.

collage Materials cut up or torn up to make a picture.

conservator Someone who cleans and repairs works of art.

engraving A print made by cutting into a steel plate with a sharp tool. Then it is printed like an etching.

etching A print made by drawing on a wax-covered metal plate. Then it is dipped in acid which eats into the part not covered by the wax. It is then inked and put through a printing press.

fibreglass material Made of fine glass shreds matted together.

fresco A painting made on to fresh plaster.

goldsmith Someone who makes gold objects.

gouge A metal instrument used for cutting into metal.

gypsum A chalky mineral used in cement, paint and Plaster of Paris.

illustrator Someone who makes drawings to explain something, such as part of a story.

impasto Very thick paint.

jade A green or greeny-grey rock.

kimono Part of Japanese traditional dress.

kinetic art Sculpture that moves.

land art Works of art inspired by the landscape or to be seen as part of the landscape.

linocut prints Made by cutting into lino, inked then printed.

lithograph A print made by transferring an image off a surface on to paper with a roller.

mineral Natural materials found in the ground such as copper.

miniature A very small painting, often a portrait.

mosaic A picture made up of tiny coloured squares called tesserae – usually stone, clay or marble – and fixed in cement.

mummy The preserved bodies of people or animals.

netsuke A Japanese carved toggle.

oil paint Pigment mixed with oil.

palette knife A flexible knife used to mix paint or spread paint on.

pigment The colour in paint.

primed A canvas that has been prepared with size and white paint (primer) ready for painting on.

relief A work of art that is between a flat painting and a three-dimensional sculpture.

sculpture A work of art that has height, width and depth.

silkscreen print A print made by forcing ink through a fine screen.

size Glue used to prepare a canvas for painting on.

sketch A quick drawing.

stencil A way of putting a shape or design on to a surface. A shape is cut out of a thin sheet of card or plastic and paint is pushed through the shape with a brush.

tempera Pigment mixed with egg yolk and water.

texture The surface of a work of art.

watercolour Pigment used with water.

woodcut A print made by cutting into blocks of wood.

Index